All About Snakes

All About Snakes

allabout
books

By Bessie M. Hecht

Illustrated by Rudolf Freund

RANDOM HOUSE
NEW YORK

FIFTH PRINTING

LIBRARY OF CONGRESS CATALOG CARD NUMBER: 56-5466

MANUFACTURED IN THE UNITED STATES OF AMERICA
BY THE HADDON CRAFTSMEN, INC., SCRANTON, PA.

All About Snakes

Contents

1

Getting Acquainted

Rare indeed is the person who doesn't jump when he comes suddenly upon a snake. And is it surprising? Snakes are among the world's strangest animals. They have no limbs. They have no familiar fur or feathers. And for thousands of years they have been stamped with an evil reputation.

It is one they really don't deserve. Of course, some snakes are dangerous and have to be looked out for. But most snakes are harmless, while a great many are even useful to man. The fact that snakes live for the most part a secret, hidden life works against them. People don't understand snakes and so have built up a lot of false notions about them.

I run into those notions every day.

"How can you pet that slimy snake?" a visitor asks me.

"Slimy?" I say. "Just pass your hand over this one."

The skin of a snake feels like finely dressed leather.

She gathers her courage and gingerly strokes the snake. A surprised look comes into her face. The feel is delightful. It is like finely dressed leather. The snake isn't slimy at all.

At this moment my pet darts out its tongue, and the woman springs back in panic. "He's trying to sting me!" she cries.

"Nonsense!" I say. "A snake can't sting with its tongue. He doesn't mean you any harm. He's just exploring the world around him. That forked tongue is his feeler. Watch how he flicks it in and out of his mouth. He is picking up odors. He places the tip of the tongue in the roof of his mouth. There is a little pocket there with a lot of nerve endings that actually do the work of smelling. A snake doesn't have any nose in the usual sense, you know. It has nostrils—those two little holes you see on either side between the tip of the snout and the eye. But it uses its nostrils only for breathing. All the smelling is done from tongue to mouth."

My visitor is somewhat reassured. "You say he doesn't mean any harm," she says. "But he looks as if he did—the way he's staring at me."

Even when a snake sleeps, his eyes are open.

All About Snakes

"How can he help staring?" I answer. "He hasn't any eyelids. See. There are just these transparent shields over his eyes—like a pair of glasses. His eyes are always open. Even when he sleeps his eyes are open."

I go on to tell her that a snake is an exceptionally wonderful creature. I say it has no external ear, yet it is not deaf, for it can feel noise vibrations through the ground. I point out that it has no paws to grasp with yet can capture prey much larger than itself.

Everything is new to my visitor. Like a great many other people she has never before thought of snakes except as something to keep away from. She feels more kindly toward them now, she says. "I'm not going to jump the next time I meet a snake," she tells me.

But I am skeptical—I know prejudice is hard to overcome. The chances are she'll jump.

2

Once They Had Legs

Just what is this strange, mysterious creature against which man has warred so long? It looks very much like a big worm as it goes crawling along. Are the two related?

Not by any means. There is a world of difference between snakes and worms. Worms haven't any backbone, while snakes most certainly have. Indeed, instead of having only twenty-six little bones in their spinal column as we do, some snakes have as many as 400. A snake's skeleton resembles a very long train of cars, with ribs or modified ribs attached to all but the first two.

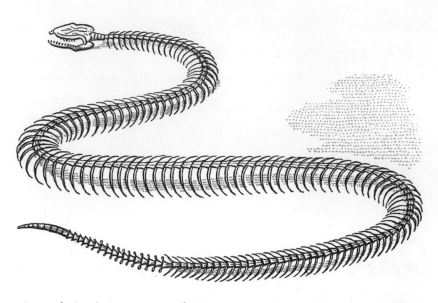

A snake's skeleton may have as many as 400 pairs of ribs.

The snake's nearest relatives are not worms but crocodiles, alligators, lizards, turtles, and the strange creature called *tuatara* that lives only on a few small islands
off New Zealand. All these animals together with snakes
make up the class we call reptiles. It is a big class, but
it isn't nearly so big as it once was.

There was a time long ago when the world was filled
with reptiles. That was in the days when dinosaurs
flourished. Then giant reptiles stomped the earth, swam
in the seas, and flapped their way on huge, batlike wings
through the sky. Those giants are all gone today. Their
descendants, the reptiles we know, are very much

shrunken in size. Even the largest of the crocodiles looks tiny beside the monstrous skeletons of some of the dinosaurs we see in the museums. Our reptiles are just an insignificant remnant of that fearful group which once roamed the earth.

Snakes are reptiles that have lost their limbs. For the snake was not always a "lowly" creature that went on its belly. In some modern boas or pythons, you can see the evidence for yourself. On each side of the under-belly, just in front of the tail, you can see two small bony structures. They are all that is left on the outside of the snake's body of what once were legs. Apparently as snakes became more specialized in their habits, they found they needed legs less and less. So with each gen-

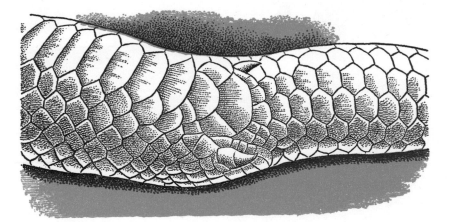

The bony points or spurs show where snakes once had legs.

In the Age of Dinosaurs, reptiles roamed the earth.

eration the legs grew smaller. Finally they disappeared. Now snakes don't even have the spurs except in a few cases.

Exactly how long ago the limbs disappeared is uncertain. But it must have happened a very long time ago. For even tens of millions of years ago snakes were pretty much like those of today. We know because they have left their skeletons in rocks that are millions of years old. Huge fossil boas and pythons have been dug up out of rocks fifty million years old. One was found in hardened volcanic ash in South America. It must have been a monster at least thirty-five feet long. Another was found in rocks of the same age in Egypt. This creature was even longer—fifty feet.

Yes, even as far back as 125 million years ago snakes had already lost their legs. For one fossil snake that was dug up in Europe came out of rocks of that age. But whenever it happened, one thing is sure—snakes get along as well without legs as many creatures with them. Snakes can crawl. Snakes can swim. Snakes can climb. Some can even glide through the air. Whatever we may think, it is no punishment to them to crawl about on their bellies.

3

Close-up View

"But what about a snake's insides?" you say. "A snake looks as if it is all tail. Does it have a heart and stomach and other organs?"

A snake does look as if it was all head and tail. But, of course, this isn't so. To know where the tail begins you have to look at the underside. Somewhere in the last half of the snake you will see a sharp difference in the arrangement of the scales. There will be a place where a series of smaller scales begins. That place marks the end of the body and the beginning of the tail. There you will see a sharply rounded scale, the anal plate, and right there you will find an opening of the body.

It is in the body part that the snake's organs are tucked away, and they are about the same as those we have. It has a heart, stomach, kidneys, liver, intestines, and—usually—just one lung. Because the snake is long and narrow, its organs are also long and narrow. And the arrangement is curious for the same reason. The parts that come in pairs, like the kidneys, don't lie side by side the way ours do. Instead they are placed one in front of the other on each side of the body. The brain, of course, is in the head. It's not a very big brain. Snakes are not intelligent in the way cats and dogs are.

Like other reptiles, snakes have neither fur nor feathers to protect them. Nevertheless they are not naked. They are covered all over with scales. These

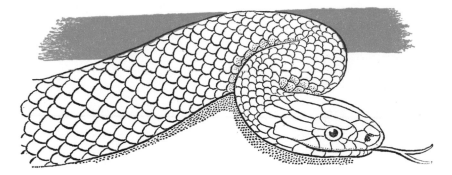

This close-up picture shows a snake's scaly covering.

may be very large. Or they may be so small that you have to look through a microscope to see them. Sometimes the scales are square. Sometimes they are round, oval, oblong, triangular or many-sided. The scales of a snake's back may be one shape, its belly scales another. And every pair of the scales on its head may be a different shape.

They are all tough and rigid. You would think such a coat was protection enough. But no. Over its scaly covering every snake wears a thin outer skin, which seems to be very important to him. Anyway, he changes it quite often. For as the snake grows, the skin gets too tight for him. Snakes keep on growing all their lives and have to have a new coat every few weeks or months. But young snakes—because they grow faster—shed their skins oftener than old ones.

It is quite a sight to see a snake shedding his old skin. The creature does it so cleverly and neatly. First he rubs his snout on a rough surface—a rock perhaps. This makes the skin around the tops of the jaws come loose. The snake keeps rubbing and pushing against the rock, and the skin starts to peel backward. As this is happening, he moves forward and crawls right out of the old skin. He is sleek and shiny now. His color pattern

This Diamond-backed Rattler will shed its skin every few weeks
or months.

looks brand new. He looks as if he had just taken a bath.

As for the skin which now lies inside out—generally in one piece—on the ground, that is a treasure for you to pick up and carry home. A snake skin is so delicate! It is as thin as tissue paper. Yet look at the skin closely and you will see the imprints of all the snake's scales. A snake expert—or herpetologist as he is called—could tell from the arrangement of the scales what kind of snake wore that coat. But possibly he would have to consult his books. For there are in the world nearly three thousand kinds of the strange and wonderful creatures we call snakes.

4

In All Kinds of Places

Whether you live in the city or on a farm, you don't have to go far to see a snake "in the wild." Even in a crowded city like New York there are still some snakes living in empty lots and undisturbed park areas.

I caught my very first snake in one such area. On a fall day when I was sixteen, my brother and I turned over a large flat rock in Van Cortlandt Park, and there the snake was—lying coiled underneath. It was a small brown creature. I knew it wasn't poisonous because I had heard there are no poisonous snakes so near New York. So I picked him up and put him in a jar I was carrying home from our picnic. Later I learned this was

A DeKay's Snake lay coiled under the large flat rock.

a DeKay's Snake. He was my pet all through the winter, but in the spring I let him go.

The United States is very rich in snakes—we have over a hundred different species. They live in all kinds of places. You will find snakes in woods, open meadows, on mountain tops, in rivers and in swamps. Some prowl in the trees and on high bushes, though they don't live there all the time. Some inhabit deserts. Some burrow underground. Off the southern coast of Florida you will even find snakes in salt water near the mouths of rivers. But in none of our coastal waters will you ever see a sea snake. Sea snakes live in tropical waters along the coasts of Asia, Africa, New Guinea and Australia. Only one sea snake has reached the New World where it lives in deep water along the west coast of Mexico, Central and South America.

Each of the different kinds of places in which a snake lives we call its *habitat*. Some snakes have just one habitat, while some—like the common Garter Snake, for instance—have several. This very common snake also has a quite large range; that is, it can be found over a wide geographical area—a big piece of the map. You will come across this snake all the way from southern Canada throughout the eastern part of the United States, and west of the Mississippi River going down into eastern Texas, Oklahoma and Kansas. Most snakes have a smaller range than this. Some have a much smaller one. The Short-tailed Snake of Florida, for example, can be found only in the central part of the state.

Now if we were to mark off on a map the range of snakes as a whole, we would find their territory is vast. But we would see at once that there are some places where snakes do not live. And we would note right away that the large areas where no snakes live are the very cold regions. There is just one kind of snake in the entire Arctic. It makes its home in northern Scandinavia. And no snake at all lives in the Antarctic. Southern Argentina is as far south as any snake has got.

"But there are Arctic foxes and polar bears," you may say. "Reindeer and whales live in the Arctic and even some birds. Why can't snakes live there?"

They cannot because snakes, like all reptiles, are cold-blooded animals. Birds and mammals, like ourselves, are warm-blooded. That means our body temperature is independent of the weather. No matter how cold it gets, the body temperature of most mammals remains about the same. But with snakes it is different. Their temperature depends a good deal on the temperature of their surroundings. If the air around them is cold, their temperature goes down. If the air around them is warm, their temperature goes up. So they cannot live in the frozen north. Indeed, snakes could not live nearly so far north and south as they do if they had not acquired the habit of hibernating.

Everybody is familiar with this word, but, no one can tell us what hibernation involves. We know that bears go into their winter quarters fat and come out in the spring lean. We say they have slept the winter away. And while sleeping, they were living at a much slower rate than they usually do. It is for this reason that they didn't need to eat for months. They used so little energy that it didn't take much fuel to keep them going. They lived off the fat already stored in their bodies.

Now, what we have said about hibernating bears is true also of snakes. But snakes hibernate for a different reason. Bears go into hibernation largely because most of their food supply is reduced. With them it is hibernate or starve. Snakes, on the other hand, go into hibernation to escape the cold. With them it is hibernate or freeze. For when the thermometer goes down, snakes find it hard to get around. At very low temperatures they can't move at all. So long as the weather is warm,

snakes are all right—they can keep comfortable by basking in the sun and crawling off into the shade when
they get too warm. But as the days get cooler, basking
isn't sufficient to keep their temperature up. Then they
have to retreat—find some place underground where
they can hibernate.

Any sort of shelter where the temperature will not go
below—or much below—freezing may be a hibernation
site. Snakes gather in caves, in holes in hills, sometimes in
burrows made by other animals, or under rotting stumps.
But the interesting thing is that the creatures don't go
looking here and there, nosing around till they find a
proper place. They may crawl back to the same hibernating den year after year.

Sometimes only one snake will be found in a shelter.
But it is very common to find a great number of snakes
using the same den. Frequently great numbers of rattle-

During cold weather snakes hibernate in holes and caves.

snakes hibernate together. Often several different kinds of snakes will be found in the same shelter with them.

For centuries, generation after generation may come back to the same crevice and go deep under the surface to hibernate.

The very cold regions of the earth are not the only ones where there is a scarcity of snakes. There are no snakes in New Zealand, and none on many of the Pacific islands. And there are no snakes in Ireland.

The story is told that St. Patrick drove them out of that country. But the truth is that by the time St. Patrick got there, there weren't any snakes in Ireland. They had all left thousands of years before, when the glaciers moved down on northern Europe. The snakes lived out the glacier period in southern Europe, where the ice didn't reach. And when it melted, some of them moved north. Before they had time to move into Ireland, however, the waters of the melting glacier had covered the land between Ireland and England. That country, too, became an island soon afterwards. And it, too, has a scarcity of snakes. There are only three kinds in the whole of England.

5

How Big? How Old?

Generally the first thing a person will tell you about any snake he has come across is how big it was. "It was *that* long!" he will say. "From here to there." That's not very exact measurement.

"But how can you measure a snake when it squirms and wriggles so?" you ask.

It is very hard. And all the harder because out in the wild where you captured it you are not likely to have a ruler handy. We hear lots of reports of snakes so many "gun-lengths" long. Many of skin length, too. But they don't help us determine how big any particular snake can get. For gun-lengths are inexact and the skin of a snake will often stretch a great deal.

I myself once had the good fortune to measure a Reticulated Python that had died recently in a zoo. I laid it out on the floor so that it was straight and measured it. It was fifteen feet long. Then I skinned it carefully and laid the skin lightly on the floor. It measured eighteen feet, or a fifth longer than the snake was.

Now, people who go to see snakes in a zoo get their greatest thrill out of seeing the pythons and Anacondas. These are the big fellows of the serpent world and everybody wants to know which is the bigger. So herpetologists went through a lot of records to find the answer. They found that the largest snake to be measured anywhere in the world was a Reticulated Python, and he was thirty-three feet long. However, since then what seems to be a reliable report has come in about an Anaconda that was thirty-eight feet long. So we really don't know which snake is bigger. The best we can do is say that the Reticulated Python is the biggest snake in the Old World and the Anaconda is the biggest snake in the New.

There are several kinds of pythons, but we can be sure that the Reticulated Python beats all the rest for size. The Indian Python of Asia and the Rock Python of Africa grow to be only about twenty-five feet long. In the New World the Boa Constrictor takes the honors for being the second largest snake. It grows to about eighteen and one-half feet. Of the world's poisonous snakes the King Cobra is the longest, reaching eighteen feet. As for the rattlers, the Eastern Diamond Back is the biggest. It grows to a little over eight feet.

Compared with all these big snakes, the burrowing blind or worm snakes—and they really do look very much like worms—seem very tiny indeed. They are so small that one can easily lie on the palm of your hand. Some grow to be no longer than a pencil and are not wider than a goose quill. These are the dwarfs of the serpent world. With the giant pythons and Anacondas at one end and worm snakes at the other, the difference in size is very striking.

Are there similar differences in the age to which snakes live?

That is a question not easy to answer. You can't tell a snake's age by looking at it, not even a rattlesnake's though many people think you can. "Just count the rattles on the end of his tail," they say. But this is wrong. A rattlesnake doesn't get one rattle a year. It adds a rattle to its tail every time it sheds its skin, and that

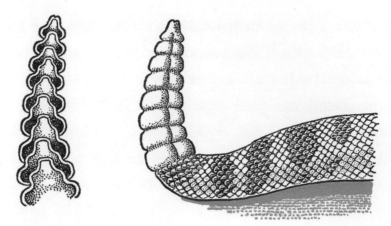

At the left is a section through the tail of a rattlesnake showing the inside of the rattle.

may be two or three times a year. The first year of its life a rattlesnake may get three rattles. After that it may add either one or two a year. Moreover, the number of rattles on a tail may not be the total that the snake has grown, for some of the segments at the tip may have broken off. They very often do.

No, the only snakes whose age you can truly tell are those that have been in captivity from birth—you know how long you have had them. Most of what is known about the ages of snakes has come out of the zoos.

The records we have are chiefly about the big snakes—the boas, the cobras, the pythons, the Anacondas, and the mambas—partly because it is these that draw the crowds and partly because the big snakes are prized

28

by the zoo people themselves. For it is hard to replace a big snake, and it costs a great deal. Naturally the big snakes get more care and attention. Records are kept about them, and from these we get most of our information about life span.

What do we know?

We know that many of the big snakes have lived in zoos for fifteen and twenty years. One cobra lived to be twenty-five years old. A South American boa—the Rainbow Snake—lived for twenty-seven years. The snake that lived the longest was an Anaconda, and it died after twenty-eight years in captivity.

An Anaconda like this lived to be twenty-eight years old.

All About Snakes

To man, who sometimes lives to a hundred, fifteen, twenty, twenty-five, and even twenty-eight years don't seem like a very long lifetime. And the life span of the big snakes seems all the more brief because they are reptiles, some of which live to a very old age. One turtle lived to be 150 years old.

Of course, living in a zoo isn't the same thing as living in the wild; so a way has been devised to check on the age of snakes that live under natural conditions. Someday we are going to know about the life span of a few snakes that live in freedom, too, because scientists have begun to gather information about them.

This is how they do it. They take individual snakes which they have caught and mark them right out in the field by clipping one or more scales under the tail. The scientists give each snake a number, mark down which scales have been clipped, weigh and measure the snake, and then release it in the exact spot in which it was found. The clipping doesn't hurt the snake and leaves a scar for future identification.

Once a year or oftener the scientist comes back to the locality and hunts for and recaptures as many of the marked snakes as he can. Then he weighs and measures them again and records his findings.

Such studies naturally are laborious and can take a good many years. So you will not be surprised that so far it is only for a few snakes that we have such records. The Western Prairie Rattlesnake is one. We have found out that at birth it weighs one ounce or less and measures seven inches. When it is a year old, it is over twenty-one inches. The second year it doesn't grow so fast, and by the time it is two years old it may be thirty-one inches long. Full grown adults may be over fifty inches. But as snakes keep growing all their lives, and as we haven't yet learned how long a Prairie Rattler can live, we can't say if this is as big as it *ever* gets.

6

Coming Into the World

Everybody knows that among birds there is often a great deal of difference between male and female in size, color, and ornamentation. With snakes this isn't the case. If you have two adults of the same snake, one male and one female and both are about the same length, you probably won't be able to tell which is which. But generally you will find that the female has a longer body and the male a longer tail. In some kinds of snakes the males will have a few very small tubercles, or knobs, on each of the scales around the base of the tail. Sometimes there are tubercles on the head and chin. Also the spurs among some of the boas and pythons are larger in the males—indeed, the females may even not have them at all.

Family life does not exist among the snakes at all, and there is no such thing as a lasting union. Sometimes you will come across two snakes together. They are together not because they live together but because food is plentiful in that particular spot. The belief that poisonous snakes travel in pairs and that if you kill one its mate will come and take revenge is a tale born of imagination.

In the Temperate Zone mating occurs in the spring after the snakes leave their hibernation dens. Sometimes two males may fight for a female. And there is likely to be a courtship dance in which the male rubs his chin on the female's neck and back. A single mating often enables the female to bear young for several years.

Parting takes place right after mating and the snakes go their independent ways, not to meet again, perhaps, except in the hibernation den. In time the female snake will lay eggs, or she may bring forth her young alive. About half the snakes do one and half the other.

As the time for egg-laying approaches, the mother snake looks around for a suitable nesting place. She may lay her eggs in a log or in rotting plant material, in

Snakes' eggs are tough and leathery rather than brittle.

sand, or perhaps in a termite nest—some place where it isn't too hot or too cold, too damp or too dry. Then generally she goes away and forgets all about them. Sometimes several females will lay their eggs in the same place, and do it year after year. In one such place as

34

many as 3,000 eggs of the European Water Snake were found.

You must not think of the eggs—which are generally white or cream-colored—as having a hard shell like birds' eggs. Snakes' eggs are tough and leathery rather than brittle. The time it takes for them to hatch differs with different kinds of snakes. If you find a snake's eggs, don't be impatient. It may take just a few days, but then again it may take as long as several months for the babies to come out.

Snakes have no sharp beaks. How then do the little ones break through the leathery shell to make their way out?

There is a special tooth—the egg tooth—by means of which the baby splits open its prison wall. The egg

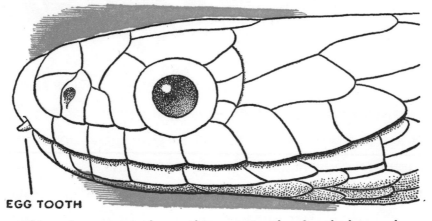

EGG TOOTH

This enlargement shows the egg tooth of a baby snake.

tooth is at the very tip of the upper jaw, set at right angles to the rest of the teeth and pointing straight ahead. This special tooth is easy to see, but unless you look for it right away, you won't see it because it falls off in a few hours, or within a day or two of the hatching.

With snakes that bear their young alive the story is even simpler. The eggs stay inside the mother's body until they are fully developed. No shell is formed around the egg—there is just a thin, clear membrane. When the time comes, the mother passes the baby snakes out of her body still wrapped in this membrane. They soon pierce it, crawl out, and are at once on their own. There is no such thing as mother looking after baby, for a baby snake is just as perfectly able to take care of itself as an adult.

This is what makes the story of the snake swallowing her young so ridiculous.

You have doubtless heard this old, old snake story, which thousands upon thousands of people believe. In times of danger, it is said, the mother snake opens her mouth and the baby snakes run down her throat. Any number of people will tell you, "I saw it with my own eyes!" But no scientist has ever seen a snake swallowing

The Garter Snake lays no eggs but brings forth living young.

her young, and every scientist will tell you it can't happen.

For, as we have said, snakes take no interest whatsoever in their young, who are perfectly able to take care of themselves. It is not likely that a snake mother will be anxious about her babies when danger threatens herself. And besides, it would be a silly snake that would, so to speak, put all her eggs in one basket and run the risk of having both herself *and* her young killed.

How then has such a myth grown up?

People *think* they see a snake swallowing its young. Perhaps what they see is a snake making a meal off some other snake; for some snakes are cannibals. Or perhaps the young crawl down a crevice near the snake's head. Or perhaps a snake is killed just about the time it is going to bear its young. Some people are taken aback when they see the babies inside a snake. "The mother must have swallowed them," they conclude. Probably they would never have said this if they had known that some snakes bring forth living young.

7

What's for Dinner?

Whether a snake is a huge python or a tiny worm snake, whether it lays eggs or bears living young, it eats the same thing—animal food. And most of it is alive.

Some snakes will eat only one kind of creature—worms, say, or fish. Others may eat only frogs. But most snakes have a combination diet—they may eat fish and frogs, or birds and mammals, or snakes and lizards. Young snakes may eat one thing, adults another. Or a snake may change its diet from season to season, eating whatever is around at the time.

It seems strange to us that snakes will eat other snakes, but there is no question that some are cannibals. Harmless kinds may eat other harmless snakes or even poisonous ones. The harmless King Snake, for instance, is a well-known rattlesnake eater. Sometimes, however, and especially in captivity, cannibalism is just a matter of accident. Two snakes may be in the same cage when food is placed before them. Both may begin swallowing the same animal, perhaps one starting at the head, the other at the tail. When the two snake heads meet, one snake will open its mouth still wider, take in the head of its cage companion, and keep right on swallowing until the whole snake is down. Once while watching two mambas eating some large rats in a zoo, I saw just this begin to happen. I called the keeper, and he separated the two before one snake had swallowed much of the other.

In capturing their prey, snakes depend a good deal on stealth. Their narrow shape and the fact that they are right down on the ground help them; they can approach without making the brush and grasses sway very much. Some snakes, indeed, will just lie and wait for something eatable to come near. But more often the serpent goes prowling around, looking for prey, inspecting holes, and peeking into nests. A Bull Snake will go right down into a gopher's hole and kill the animal in its own lair.

A keen sense of smell and good eyesight also help most snakes in their hunting. But some are endowed with a strange special sense. It is a sense which enables them to "feel" when a warm-blooded animal comes near. And this, you can readily see, is a great advantage when hunting for food in the dark.

Some boas and pythons, as well as rattlesnakes, copperheads, moccasins, and all the other snakes which we call pit-vipers have this sense. For a long time scientists were greatly puzzled by the pits in the heads of these snakes. In the pit-vipers these pits are located one on each side of the head between the nostril and the eye. In the boas and pythons they are located in some of the scales along the lower jaw. Scientists knew that these pits must carry important information to the snakes because large nerves lead from the pits to the brain. But they couldn't imagine what that information might be. Now we know.

Here is how we can demonstrate what the pits do for a snake:

We blindfold a rattlesnake, or some other snake that

The blindfolded rattlesnake strikes out at the hot balloon.

has pits, by putting tape over each eye. Next we take two balloons. We fill one with cool water and another with hot water. Then we suspend them one at a time in front of the blindfolded snake. The snake will pay little attention to the cold balloon, but he will strike directly at the hot one and burst it. He has "felt" the warmth of the hot balloon. And he strikes out in that direction just as he would strike at a warm-blooded mouse that approached him in the dark.

Now, snakes are provided with teeth, but these teeth

are not intended for chewing. Snakes swallow their food whole. You may well ask how they can do it when often the prey is so much wider than the snake's throat. A snake with a neck no thicker than a man's finger can easily swallow a large rat. A python is able to swallow a sixty-pound pig, a goat, or an antelope; and pythons have been known to swallow even leopards and human beings. How do they manage it?

They manage it because their heads are especially adapted for swallowing prey whole. All the bones of the head are joined very loosely. This means that the head can stretch and the mouth can take in prey that is four or five times as wide as the snake's head is normally.

The manner in which a snake goes about this remark-

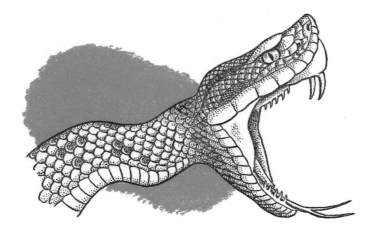

The head and mouth of a snake can stretch enormously.

able feat is quite astonishing. The snake opens his mouth wide and sinks his teeth into the prey. Generally it is the snout he seizes, and for a time he just holds on. The teeth, being curved backward, hook in very firmly; so the harder the prey struggles to get free, the firmer the teeth hold. After a while, when the prey decides it's useless to struggle any more and submits to its fate, the snake starts swallowing. Slowly he moves one side of the head forward, then the other. Upper and lower jaws work together, but only half of each jaw moves at one time. It looks as if the snake is slowly crawling over his food. And it looks as if he is working terribly hard. His eyes bulge. His head stretches so you wonder if it will ever be right again.

It may take only a few minutes for the snake to finish off his victim. But if the prey is big and bulky in shape, it may take a few hours. And if the process is long, the snake will stop regularly to breathe. Normally he breathes through his nostrils and the air goes down the windpipe. But if he is long swallowing his prey, the windpipe is blocked by the food. So the snake stretches the forward part of his windpipe under the prey and lets the windpipe stick out of his mouth so as to get air to the lungs directly.

A snake can swallow prey bigger than its own head

All About Snakes

It is not exactly what we would call dainty eating, and it may not be much fun. The snake's pleasure must come only afterwards in the sense of having satisfied his hunger. But it is a question just how comfortable a snake feels right after his meal when with bulging stomach he lies low and takes time out to digest his meal.

That process may take anywhere from two to ten days. Snakes digest everything that goes down except hair, feathers, teeth, claws and horns. And the meal is enough for a long time. We don't know, of course, how often they eat in the wild, but in captivity snakes are fed only once every two or three weeks. For they are sluggish animals and don't require as much food as creatures that move around a lot. There are many records of snakes not eating for months and even a year or more. And there is one record of a snake—a Madagascar boa—that didn't eat for four years!

Seizing prey by the snout and swallowing it alive is as primitive a way of getting your food as there is. But not all snakes do it this way. Two groups of snakes have a less direct approach—they kill their prey first.

One group does it by squeezing the prey to death, or *constricting* it, as we say. A number of our native snakes constrict by throwing merely one coil around the ani-

Some snakes squeeze their prey to death before eating it.

mal. Powerful constrictors like the boas and pythons, however, generally throw several coils around the animal. They tighten the coils and tighten them—till all movement stops. Many people believe that the victim's bones are crushed in the process, but this isn't so. What the squeezing does is make it impossible for the lungs to breathe and the heart to beat. When the heart stops, the snake knows he'll get no more resistance and, uncoiling, starts swallowing the victim usually head first.

The second group of snakes that kill their prey before they swallow it are the poisonous or *venomous* snakes. They inject into the victim a poisonous fluid we call *venom*.

Behind each eye all venomous snakes have a gland which manufactures this venom. But it is in the snakes we call vipers and pit-vipers that the mechanism which injects the venom is best developed. A little canal leads from the gland to a hollow tooth, or *fang*, in the front part of the upper jaw. At the moment the snake strikes, the venom flows into the canal, through the hollow tooth, and into the victim. The mechanism is very remarkable. It works exactly like a hypodermic needle—a device which snakes developed tens of millions of years before man invented his own hypodermic needle.

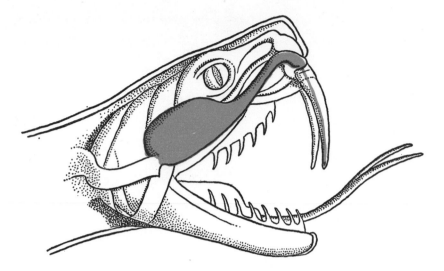

The snake's venom, shown in color, flows through the fang.

The snake's device is a miracle of efficiency. The serpent strikes at its prey and bites. The biting creates a pressure on the gland, and instantly the venom starts flowing. The whole thing happens with lightning speed. For the snake to strike, bite, inject the venom, and return his head to its ordinary defense position may take *less than half a second!*

8

Danger!

It was time to feed the baby rattlesnake again. He was one of four Timber Rattlers born in the laboratory and ate readily every time I fed him. I dropped a mouse into the cage. At once the little snake started to rattle, and like a flash he struck. The mouse took a few steps, then fell over on his side. In a few minutes he was dead.

What did the venom do to make the little mouse die so quickly? And does the venom of all snakes act the same way?

Different venoms affect animals differently. One venom may destroy the blood corpuscles and the small blood vessels so that the creature bleeds to death inside.

That's what happened to the little mouse. Another venom may affect the nervous system, quickly destroying the parts of the brain that control breathing. With such venoms death is generally even faster. Or the venom may affect both the blood *and* the nervous system, which is what most snake venoms do.

Human beings are, of course, affected the same way as animals, but luckily people don't always die when they are bitten by a venomous snake. For the power, or as we say the *potency*, of venoms differs. And an amount of venom that is enough to kill a small animal is generally not enough to kill a human being. It is only when the venom is very potent that snake bite can kill a man.

Now, we have to admit that in the world there are many snakes that have that potent kind of venom, a single drop of which will kill a human being. Yet the danger from snakes is not nearly so great as people think. Of course, in a country like India, where many go barefoot and where to certain people some of the deadly snakes are sacred animals that mustn't be killed, death from snake bite is common. In that country some 10,000 people may die of it every year.

But in the United States we wear shoes; so snake bite

isn't common at all. And extremely few people die even
when they are bitten. For except for the Coral Snake,
which is small and secretive and so isn't very trouble-
some anyway, our venomous serpents—rattlesnakes,
moccasins, and copperheads—don't have the most potent
kind of venom. Our most dangerous snake is the Western Diamond Rattlesnake because its venom, while not
the worst there is, is quite potent. But rattlesnakes fortunately give a warning rattle; so often there is time to
get out of the way. Many more people in this country
are bitten by copperheads than by any other venomous
snake, and the bite of a copperhead is very seldom fatal.

Today there aren't nearly so many deaths from snake
bite the world over as there were just a few years ago.
For now we have a remedy against snake bite. Serum
has been developed to counteract snake venom.

To make this lifesaving serum, a small amount of
snake venom is first injected into horses. Over several
months bigger and bigger doses are injected. The horses'
resistance to the venom is slowly built up until finally
it doesn't affect them any more. They become immune
to it, as we say. Some of the horses' blood is then drawn
off and a serum is made out of a certain part of it. A
person who has been bitten by a venomous serpent can

have the serum injected into himself so that the snake's venom may be neutralized.

There is a different serum for different kinds of snake venom. In Asia the lives of thousands of people bitten by cobras have been saved by a cobra serum. In Brazil there is a serum against the bite of the Bushmaster and another for the Jararaca and its relatives. Still others are for the Tropical Rattlesnake and the Coral Snake. Because of all these remedies, death from snake bite in Brazil has been cut by more than half.

In our country we have never had more than about 100 deaths a year. And since anti-venomous serum was developed, we have no more than ten to twenty deaths a year. The serum we use is not for any one kind of venom. Our serum is a combination against the poisons of rattlesnakes, the copperhead, and the Water Moccasin. A person bitten by a Coral Snake will not be helped by the serum. But so few are bitten by this deadly creature that it hasn't seemed worth-while to develop a serum against its poison.

You might ask how we get the snake venom in the first place when we want to make serum. We get it by "milking" snakes.

I myself once helped "milk" some moccasins. We

The venom from the moccasin can be "milked" into a glass.

picked the snakes up carefully behind the head and forced open the mouth. Then we held the upper jaw directly over a cup which was covered by a tightly stretched piece of cloth. The snake bit into the cloth and the venom ran down into the cup. We squeezed the poison glands while "milking" so as to get as much venom as possible out of each snake.

The venom itself looks perfectly harmless—you would never suspect it to be so dangerous. It is just a clear, thick, whitish or yellowish liquid. It spoils readily, but when dried it forms into a crystal-like solid that remains potent for years.

What should you do to prevent being bitten by a venomous snake? And what should you do if you do get bitten?

In the first place, you should learn what kinds of snakes there are in your particular region and whether any of them are venomous. Then you should find out what the venomous kinds look like. For there is no one way to tell a venomous snake from harmless ones, though some people think there is. "Look at the head," they will tell you. "If it is triangular, the snake is poisonous." That isn't true. Some venomous snakes do have triangular heads, but many do not. The best way to get acquainted with the venomous snakes in your region is to visit the nearest zoo or museum—and at the same time you can learn to recognize the harmless kinds, too.

Then, when you go out into places where you may come across a venomous snake, wear heavy shoes, or preferably boots. And if you are hiking in rocky places, watch where you put your unprotected hands. It is a good idea, too, to carry a First Aid Snake Bite Outfit in your pocket.

If you are bitten—which is very unlikely provided you are careful—don't get panicky. In the first place, it may not have been a venomous snake that bit you. If nothing happens within ten minutes of the bite, you can be sure the snake was harmless. For a bite from a venomous serpent takes effect quickly. In a few minutes there is a burning pain and soon there is a distinct swelling. However, even if you are sure it was a venomous snake that bit you, or if pain develops, still you don't have to get panicky. Remember that death from snake bite in this country is extremely rare. Start working on the bite.

The first thing to do is to prevent the venom from getting very far. You can do it by making a tourniquet —that is, by tying any narrow, flexible material between the bite and the heart. A tourniquet will prevent the venom—or very much of it—from going to the rest of the body.

Once the tourniquet is in place, cuts should be made over the fang marks to let out the venom at the place of the bite. A one-edged razor blade is the best instrument for this. Then someone should suck out the venom.

This may be done by mouth, but the person doing it *must have no cuts in his mouth*. For venom does no harm if it is swallowed; it has harmful effects only when it gets into the bloodstream directly through a cut. Or the venom may be drawn out by applyng a suction cup that comes with a First Aid Snake Bite Outfit. Meantime a doctor should be urgently sent for. He will continue the suction and will give you other treatment—such as anti-venomous serum—as it is needed.

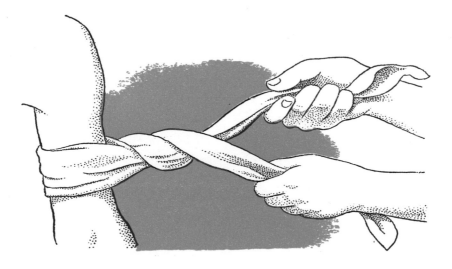

9

The Burrowers

There are so many kinds of snakes in the world! How can anybody get to know them all?

It would be a job indeed if you had to get acquainted with each one separately. Fortunately it isn't necessary. Scientists have grouped snakes into different families, and you can learn the characteristics of a whole family all at one time. For as with other families, the members of a snake family may be quite different and yet in some very significant ways they will be alike.

You want to be able to say, "This snake is a pit-viper for such and such reasons." Or "This is one of the boas because it has this and that." So let us get acquainted with some of the families. And let us begin with those of the burrowing snakes, for they are perhaps the oldest snakes on earth. Certainly they are the most primitive.

These little fellows are more like worms than snakes. Some, indeed, are not much bigger than a good-sized angleworm. The largest will get to be three feet long, but the average is ten or twelve inches. To one family of these little wormlike snakes scientists have given a Greek name which means *blind eyes*. The little creatures aren't really blind, however. It is only that their eyes are nearly hidden by their scales. That's for protection —because they are burrowers. In some kinds you can just barely see two dark spots which are the eyes.

There are numerous species of blind snakes, and many of them are so much alike that you would not be able to tell one from another. Even a herpetologist would have to study the arrangement of the head scales and count the rows of scales around the body before he could tell to which species it belonged. And right here it might be as well to say what we mean by *species*. We say that two animals belong to the same species if they will mate with one another and produce young which in turn will be able to reproduce themselves.

Blind snakes are found all over the world in tropical

areas. When I was collecting reptiles in the West Indies
for the American Museum of Natural History, I found
a number of blind snakes. I dug them out of termite
nests. I also found them under well-rotted logs of coconut palms. The little West Indian burrowers looked like
shining silvery worms. The scales over their bodies were
highly polished, smooth, rounded and overlapping—just
right for a burrowing creature. For the same reason the
scales all over the body were of the same size, too, not,
as in most snakes, larger on the belly. There were very
few teeth, and all were in the upper jaw.

We found burrowing snakes under rotted coconut logs.

When I would get the blind snakes out of their hiding places, they would immediately try to escape by burrowing into the soil. They were amazingly quick, and I had to act fast to keep them from getting away from me. If I took one up, it would turn away from the light and try to burrow into my hand.

I kept the captives in fine sand in a cage with a sliding glass front. Blind snakes like moist soil; so I moistened the sand a little every day. The little fellows stayed buried in it all day long, but during the night they would come up to feed. They ate the larvae and adults of the tiny Common Flour Beetle and the Large Flour Bettle. The snakes thrived on this diet. And this surprised me; for the natural food of blind snakes is termites, grubs, young earthworms, centipedes and sometimes small snake eggs.

One morning I found some of the shed skin on top of the sand. I had never seen the shed skin of a blind snake before and examined it curiously. It was not all in one piece like the snake skins I was used to seeing. Instead, each ring of scales running around the body was separate. The rings had been shed one by one and looked like a series of overlapping but unconnected cigar bands.

The heads of blind snakes are very small and their

tails are the same shape as the head; so the burrowers are often called two-headed snakes. At the end of the tail a short spine sticks out, which the little snakes use to prick whoever handles them. This habit terrifies some native people. "Blind snakes have a sting in their tail!" they say. But this is not so.

Nearly all the blind snakes lay eggs. Some of these are not more than half an inch long and a sixth of an inch wide and look like grains of cooked rice.

Because the members of this family of snakes are so small and because they burrow into the soil, sometimes they get accidentally carried far away from their home area. A few of these accidental immigrants may even have taken a trip in potted plants to the United States. But our country is not within their normal range.

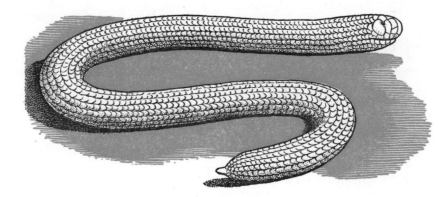

A short spine is at the end of a blind snake's tail.

Yet we have a family of blind snakes here, too. They are so much like the family that lives in the tropics that only an expert can tell them apart. One way is by the teeth—our worm snakes have teeth only on the *lower* jaw.

There are two species of worm snakes here, and both are found in the Southwest—from Kansas and Texas west to California. The largest of these worm snakes gets to be a little over a foot long. They look somewhat transparent and are whitish pink in color. Like their tropical and subtropical cousins, they are excellent burrowers. Sometimes when construction work is going on, a bulldozer will accidentally dig some up. Then everybody crowds around to see the snakes that look so much like worms. For the burrowers spend so much time underground that people don't see them much, though some of the little snakes live in gardens. At dusk, or possibly in the early morning, they come to the surface to feed. Many then crawl out on the roads, and in the evening hundreds are killed by cars.

10

The Boa Family

Let us now jump from the smallest to the largest snakes, those around which people crowd at the zoo.

The boas and the pythons both belong to the boa family, and there is no easy way to tell one from the other. A herpetologist can tell by the skull and other indications which is which, but you will not be faced with the problem because you will not run across any pythons in our country. All the pythons, except one that is found in Mexico and Central America, live in the Old World.

Now, what do the boas and pythons have in common that has made scientists put them in one family?

64

Most of them have spurs, which as we said before, are remains of what once were legs. All kill their prey by constriction. None has fangs. And the scales of all are similar: on the back and sides they are small, on the belly there is a row of large ones. Of course, most other snakes have enlarged scales on the belly, too, but in the boa family the scales are much narrower in proportion to their size.

The Reticulated Python is king of the pythons. This huge snake lives in Malaya, the Philippines, southern China and Burma. It is a very handsome snake with an intricate pattern of yellow, brown, and black scales that reminds you of some Oriental rugs. Wild tales are told about the swallowing feats of this big snake. You have probably heard that it can swallow an ox. But this is not true. Though snakes can stretch their mouths amazingly, not even the largest snake could swallow an ox.

Nevertheless, the Reticulated Python is a dangerous snake and people are right to fear it, for there are some true stories of its overcoming human beings.

Some of these dangerous snakes are very heavy, weighing as much as 250 pounds. When they travel, they leave a wide trail that can be followed easily. One naturalist in Borneo followed the trail of what must have

A Reticulated Python is so heavy that it may leave a trail of broken plants and branches as it travels.

been a giant Reticulated Python. The plants it had crawled over had been bent down flat by its weight. A piece of dead wood over which the snake had gone was broken and pressed into the ground. As the serpent came close to a stream, he had scraped the moss off the trunk of a tree and had left impressions on the sandy shore as if a heavy sack of grain had been dragged over the bank. The man never did see the python, for it was hiding in the stream. But it might very well have been even bigger than the thirty-three foot snake that is the longest python on record.

Poultry and swine are what Reticulated Pythons often eat, and these are what they are fed in the zoos—freshly killed chickens or pigs. After the snakes have eaten, they often crawl into their bathing tank. And there they may stay for a week digesting their meal.

When you see them lying gorged and very still, you would never suspect that these great, heavy snakes are nervous animals. But they are. They are upset when they are made captive. When first brought in, they will often refuse to eat. Sometimes a python will fast for eight or ten months and will actually starve to death unless he is made to eat.

The pythons which you see in the snake-charming

act at the circus or in the traveling shows are not Reticulated Pythons. The Reticulated Python is not hardy enough to go through all that a circus snake has to endure. He is not a good traveler. Commonly it is the Indian Python that you see the snake charmer wind about her arms and neck and body. Though nervous and vicious when first taken captive, the Indian Python soon calms down and becomes a good trouper.

In his native jungle home, the Indian Python is a good tree climber. He may climb up in a tree and stay motionless for a long time. Then when an unsuspecting monkey gets too close, there is a sudden swish and the monkey finds himself in the snake's coils. The Indian Python will eat monkeys or any other living thing he can get, be it jackal, porcupine, rat, frog, lizard or deer. The last he swallows down, horns and all. He has even been known to eat leopards.

Africa has its pythons as well as Asia. The largest is the Rock Python, which grows to twenty-five feet. In most movies of African animals you will see this snake, and generally you will see natives showing great fear of it. It is with good reason they are afraid. For there are true stories of Rock Pythons killing people. One comes from a region where it is against the people's

him. He would never make any sudden movements and would sit perfectly still in your hand. He liked to hide under a piece of bark or in his bed of sawdust. At night he would come out and feed on the small mice I gave him.

Another boa was one I got just by chance. It was a Bahaman boa and had come to New York on a banana boat. It had been found by the men who were unloading the bananas. Luckily they were men with strong curiosity, and instead of killing the snake, as most people would, they brought it to the American Museum of Natural History to be identified. I was on the Museum staff at that time. The men were very glad to hear it wasn't venomous. They made us a present of the snake, and I kept it alive for several months, feeding it small mice. He would feed at night; but sometimes, if I covered the cage to make it dark for him, he would eat during the day.

Nearly all boas are tropical animals, but there are two kinds of boas in our country, too, both in the West. The Rubber Boa, which gets its name because its brown, yellow, or gray scaly skin looks rubbery, is a small burrowing snake that grows to eighteen inches. It lives in the forests and mountains of some of the Rocky

All About Snakes

Mountain states west to California and has been found as far up as 10,000 feet. This little secretive snake will roll right up into a ball when it is frightened.

The other boa in our country is called the Rosy Boa. It lives in southern California, southwestern Arizona and Mexico, and it, too, likes to hide itself. You will recognize this little snake by three zigzag reddish brown or pink stripes running all the way from nose to tail. The base color is a bluish gray, and this, together with the smooth and shiny scales, makes the Rosy Boa look as if it was made of metal. It is gentle and makes a nice pet.

Most of the boas in the world bear living young, and lots of them at a time. A great many baby boas have been born in our zoos. One Anaconda gave birth to thirty-four young all at one time. Another bore thirty-seven. A Boa Constrictor gave birth to sixty-four babies. But the record birth is bigger still. An Anaconda nineteen feet long and three feet around gave birth to seventy-two young! And each baby snake was over three feet long!

The pythons also have many young. But they all hatch out of eggs, for no python bears living young. Fifty to a hundred eggs are laid at one time. A python mother shows more interest in her eggs than most other snakes do. She coils about them and stays that way for six or eight weeks till the eggs hatch. But once the young ones have left their shells, she pays no attention to them at all.

A python mother coils about her eggs until they hatch.

11

Just Ordinary Snakes

Two-thirds of all the snakes in the world belong to a single family! So you will not be surprised to find it called *Colubridae*, which means simply snakes, and which we might call typical snakes. Most of them are harmless. Some, however, do have poison fangs.

Of the snakes you find, the great majority will be typical snakes, and yet they will be very different from one another in size and form and color and habits. Some will be long and thin. Others will be short and stout. Some will be dull in color, others will be ablaze with it. Some will live in trees and on bushes. Others will live in the water, on the ground or under it. Some will lay eggs, and some will bring forth living young.

Typical snakes live all over the world, wherever snakes can live, but some kinds you will never find in our country. You will never find any Wart Snakes, for instance. Until the Second World War, I myself never saw a Wart Snake, and even then it was only a preserved specimen in a bottle.

It happened like this. During the war we often received packages at the Museum from soldiers who had collected and preserved animals for study. Whenever such a package arrived, we opened it with great excitement. On account of wartime secrecy, the soldiers were not allowed to tell us where they were; so it was a kind of game for us to guess where the animals had come from. The Wart Snake arrived in one such package from "nowhere."

The creature looked very ugly and queer to me. Its head was very short. The nostrils and small eyes were on top of its head. Little ridged scales encircled the whole body.

Had the specimen come from Asia? I got down some books on Pacific snakes and started to leaf through them. And soon I found a picture of the serpent in the bottle.

All About Snakes

I started to read. The Wart Snake, I learned, is a completely aquatic snake—that is, a snake living entirely in the water. Its home is in streams and even salt water, and, being a ravenous fish-eater, it often gets caught in fishermen's nets. Its range is India, Indo-China, the Indo-Australian region, and northern Australia to the Solomon Islands.

This being quite a wide area, I didn't even try to guess where the snake had been collected. Not till the war was over did I learn that it had been picked up in New Guinea.

Unlike the Wart Snake, our water snakes are only semi-aquatic, living in the water only part of the time. Their eyes and nostrils are on the sides, not the top, of the head. The snout is rounded. And instead of little scales all the way around, water snakes have enlarged scales on the belly.

There are ten different kinds of water snakes in our country. The ugly Brown Water Snake is the largest and may grow to five feet, though the average water snake is less than three feet long. Water snakes may be banded, blotched or striped, and sometimes the belly may have a colorful pattern. While nearly all the species feed on fish, some eat slugs and earthworms, and one

The nostrils of a water snake are on the sides of its head.

seems to eat almost nothing but crayfish. Most of the water snakes have one very unpleasant habit—when they are disturbed, their scent glands release a disagreeable odor and a sticky substance. This habit, together with the fact that some are quite aggressive and look much like moccasins, makes people believe water snakes are venomous. But they are not. They are harmless.

In Europe and Asia there are even more kinds of water snakes than in the United States. One—the Grass Snake—is among the commonest snakes in Europe. But here is something curious. Nearly all the water snakes of the Old World lay eggs, while all of ours give birth to living young.

The little brown snakes which you are so apt to see are close relatives of the water snakes. If you live in the city, you may find one in a vacant lot under trash. It will doubtless be a DeKay's Snake, for that is a common place for them to be. If, on the other hand, you go to the woods and find a little brown snake under bark and fallen trees, it is more likely to be the Red-Bellied Snake. The two snakes are about the same size— usually less than a foot long. The red belly and gray back of one and the dark spots on the back of the other will tell you which snake you have found.

Commonest of all the snakes in our country is a relative of both the water and the brown snakes. This is the Garter Snake. You are almost certain to find it if you are on the lookout for snakes because it lives in every state of the Union—and in great numbers. Usually the creature will be a dull green, gray, or brown, with one or more light stripes on the body. In the United States there are eleven different kinds of Garter Snakes, and sometimes you will find more than one species in the same place.

I have found a vast number of Garter Snakes in my

Evidently this was the entrance to a mass hibernation den.

life. Once early in the spring I went out to an open area on the outskirts of New York City where I knew Garter Snakes lived. It was a big, open lot with many layers of large flat rocks that made an excellent shelter for snakes. And there, emerging from a deep crevice was a mass of entwined Garter Snakes. Others were lying on top of rocks sunning themselves. Evidently this was the entrance to a mass hibernation den, and I had come upon the snakes as they were coming out. I caught a few of the larger ones and put them in a sack to take to the Museum. The chances were that the snakes had mated, and we wanted to see how many young would be in a brood. As the snakes began to retreat under the rocks, I tried to make a quick count of how many there were. I couldn't do it, but I estimated I had seen at least a hundred.

Of those that I carried to the Museum, three females gave birth in July. The broods had five, twelve, and twenty young. Some of the babies learned to eat chopped meat, others would eat only earthworms, while two refused to eat anything. When I saw that I would not be able to raise them, I took those two back where I had found their mothers.

Hog-nosed Snakes are another of our common harm-

The Hog-nosed Snake can look as threatening as a cobra.

less snakes that I have often found. In the spring I would see them in a sandy region on the south shore of Long Island. "What wicked-looking creatures they are!" I would think as I surveyed their short, thick bodies and flattened heads with upturned snouts. Sometimes when I would come upon one suddenly, it would hiss and inflate its lung with air. This would flatten the front part of its body so that it looked very threatening and cobra-like. Then I would think, "No wonder people believe it is venomous! No wonder they call up the Museum to ask if there are any cobras around New York!"

The Hog-nosed Snakes are sometimes called Spreading Adders on account of this inflating trick. But it is all bluff. There is no harm in a Hog-nosed Snake. Toads and frogs and insects are their only diet, and the ugly upturned snout is just for digging.

Another harmless bluffer that hisses quite loudly and even vibrates his tail to make a rattling noise is the Pine Snake. I have seen them in the pine barrens of southern New Jersey. One I caught was a full-grown

The Pine Snake is another harmless bluffer.

adult. He had many dark blotches on his light gray body and was about four feet long. I let him coil around my arm and could feel how he must constrict his prey. Then I uncoiled him and let him go. Later that day, while driving along in the same region, I found another one. It was a female that had been hit by a car. There was a huge gash in her side, and I could see eight eggs that looked as if they were about to be laid.

Pine Snakes range from southern New Jersey south to Florida and west to Texas. They are also very common through the Great Plains and deserts from Texas to California, but in that region they are called Bull Snakes or Gopher Snakes.

12

More Typical Snakes

One spring day while hunting for snakes in central New York State, I saw two of our more colorful northeastern snakes. They were the Ring-necked Snake and the Smooth Green Snake. Both were lying coiled under large slabs of rock where the earth was moist and cool. The body of the Ring-necked Snake was dark, almost black, with a brilliant yellow band around its neck. The belly was the same yellow color. I knew that not all Ring-necked Snakes are colored like this and that in some the belly might be red or orange, with black spots down the center or on the sides, perhaps. But the ring of bright color around the neck made me sure it was a

Ring-necked Snake, for nearly all have some kind of brilliant coloring there. I didn't take the snake away because in captivity it doesn't eat readily and is not an easy snake to keep.

The Smooth Green Snake had a brilliant green body with a creamy white belly and chin. It was about a foot long. I hated to leave it because it was so pretty. But I knew it would not do well as a pet, and after taking a color picture, I let it go.

It was not till several years later, when I was on my way to Florida on a collecting trip, that I saw my first Rough Green Snake. This is a cousin of the Smooth Green Snake and gets the name *Rough* on account of the little ridges on its scales. The one I found was about two feet long, yet I almost didn't see it; for it was sitting in a small bush almost hidden by the leaves.

During that collecting trip in Florida I had a very lucky find. I was walking through a wooded area, mostly to get out of the hot sun, when I saw a rotting log lying across my path. I tried to turn it over. But it was so decayed that it split down the middle. And there in the middle was a hollow with eleven eggs in it. I saw, of course, by their soft leathery look that they were snake eggs.

The Eastern Coachwhip may be over eight feet long.

Because of their size, I knew they had been laid by one of the larger snakes of the region, such as the Chicken, Black, or Indigo Snake. But I had no way of knowing which one. I gathered them together with some of the moist, rotting wood and put them carefully in a box. Later I put moist moss on top of the eggs. Several weeks later, after I had brought them to New York, the first hatchling appeared, and my curiosity was satisfied. The little snake had a pattern of light and dark saddles, and I recognized it at once as the young of the Black Snake.

Black Snakes are found throughout our country. They are easy to recognize because they are all black when adult and their scales have a luster like gun metal. They grow to be four to five feet long. The Racers, which are common in the West, are their close relatives. They average four feet, but the Eastern Coachwhip, which is also a Racer, grows to be about eight and a half feet. It is among the largest of the non-venomous snakes in the United States and looks very much like a braided whip.

Almost a year after my Florida egg find, I was in Canada. One day on the northern shore of Lake Ontario, about a hundred feet from the water, I came upon a large rotting log that looked to me like a good nesting place for snakes. Just for fun, I kicked at it. A slab fell off, revealing a groove filled with discolored eggs. Before I could recover from my surprise, I saw young snakes about a foot long pouring out right and left from the exposed crevices. With both hands I grabbed them, leaving the eggs to be picked up later. Before I got through, I had stuffed a sack with more than fifty baby Fox Snakes.

The whole log was riddled with eggs. Some, of course, were empty, for the young had hatched out of them. But the others looked as if they would hatch shortly. A count of hatched and unhatched eggs showed

More than 200 Fox Snake eggs had been laid in this log.

that more than 200 had been laid in this log. Several females had used it as their nesting place.

Fox Snakes, which grow to be over five feet long, have relatives all over the country. In the East there are the Pilot Black Snakes, in the West the Rat Snakes, in the South the Chicken Snakes. These last get their name because they are often found around chicken coops and barns, where they hunt for rats and mice.

Milk Snakes also get their name from the fact that they stay around barns—cow barns. And they stay there for the same reason that Chicken Snakes are found around chicken coops and barns—to hunt rats and mice. To be sure, Chicken Snakes will sometimes eat young chickens and eggs. But nothing of that sort can be said about Milk Snakes—they don't drink milk. Nevertheless, some people foolishly insist the snakes do and that they suck it from the cows. This is impossible. Snakes have no sucking muscles and couldn't drink in this manner. Nor is milk something a snake could digest. Its system is not geared for the digestion of liquid or sticky food. Milk would just run through the snake's intestine without doing the creature any good.

Milk Snakes range east of the Rocky Mountains and southward into Mexico to Central America. They are handsome snakes with their black-bordered, irregular red or chestnut blotches on the back and their checkered black and white bellies. They grow to an average of about two and a half feet. Their relatives the King Snakes grow somewhat larger and are just as handsome.

All About Snakes

They are cannibals, feeding on snakes of other species. Some even eat rattlesnakes, and if bitten in the process, are not poisoned, for they are immune to the rattlesnake's venom. Strangely enough, King Snakes are very docile toward man and make excellent pets.

Perhaps you have heard about the snake that can take its tail in its mouth and roll down a hill like a hoop. Actually there are two snakes about which this story is told—the Mud Snake and the Rainbow Snake, both living in our South. There is no truth in the silly story whatsoever. Many years age, herpetologists at the

Sometimes a King Snake will devour a rattlesnake.

Chicago Museum of Natural History offered $1,000 to anyone who brought in a snake that would perform this feat. Needless to say, no one has produced such a serpent.

It is also said that these snakes have a sting at the end of the tail. I have never caught a Mud Snake, but I handled a Rainbow Snake in a zoo once. There is a spine at the tip of the tail. I pressed it into the palm of my hand, and the spine didn't hurt or sting.

The Rainbow Snake is a very beautiful creature. Its body color is a glittering purple cut by narrow bright red stripes. The sides have orange bands, and the scales are red-tipped while the belly is red with rows of purple dots. In Florida it is common to find this snake five feet long.

Color is brilliant among many of the desert snakes in our Southwest. The Leaf-nosed, Long-nosed, Patch-nosed, and Shovel-nosed Snakes are all colorful. Some of these snakes were long considered very rare. But when collectors started driving along roads at night to look for snakes, they discovered their mistake—and why they had made it. In one area the snake which was thought to be the rarest proved to be the most common. Most of the desert snakes come out at night to avoid the intense heat of the day.

Among the desert snakes you will see some very curious snouts. They are specially shaped so the snakes can use them as a shovel. One of the best adapted is that of the Banded Sand Snake—it really is shaped like a shovel. The scales of the short, heavy body are highly polished, too, to help the snake glide easily through the sand. The creature crawls just beneath the surface. As he passes along, the sand on top caves in, leaving a groove-like track.

Now, all the typical snakes we have been talking about are harmless. But about one-third of the family

The Banded Sand Snake crawls just beneath the surface.

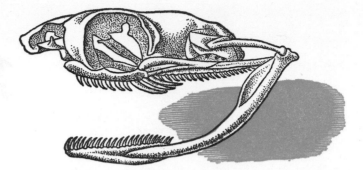

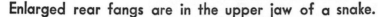

Enlarged rear fangs are in the upper jaw of a snake.

do have fangs. These fangs are not hollow teeth as in the rattlesnake but are merely grooved along the front. The poison runs down the groove and into the prey. The fangs are not in the front of the mouth but in the back; so we call these snakes *rear-fanged snakes*. Only a few of them live in this country, and all are in the Southwest. The Lyre Snake, the Cat-eyed Snake, the Blackbanded Snake, and the Vine Snake are all rear-fanged.

These snakes do not strike their prey and withdraw as certain others of the venomous snakes do. Usually the rear-fanged snakes hold on and use a chewing action to get the rear grooved teeth into the prey, which may be small mammals, lizards or frogs. None of our rear-fanged snakes is dangerous to man. But the Bloomslang, a rear-fanged snake of Africa, can give a serious bite.

13

Venom Is Their Weapon

After the gaint boas and pythons the most popular snakes at the zoo are the cobras and mambas. Everyone is curious to see these deadly venomous serpents that figure so often in folk tales and travelers' stories. For who has not heard of the cobra that spreads a hood and the mamba that shoots like chain lightning from a tree?

Together with the Coral Snakes and a few others, the cobras and mambas make up a single family. And what they all have in common is their teeth. All have *short*, rigid, hollow fangs in the *front* part of the mouth.

This sensational family lives on every continent inhabited by snakes except Europe. The New World has only the Coral Snakes. But Africa and southern Asia are infested with members of the family, while in Australia every poisonous snake—and there are many—belongs to it.

There are more than a dozen different kinds of cobras, more than half of them in Africa. Yet whenever we think of cobras, it is the image of the Spectacled Cobra of India that comes first to our minds. For this is the snake used by the Indian snake charmers.

Let us sit in on a performance and get a glimpse of the famous serpent that thrills even more people than it kills.

Perhaps we will find the snake charmer at his regular stand under the trees of a public square. Or perhaps we will see him walking along a village street with a lot of excited children behind him. They know that there are cobras in his flat baskets and that as soon as a large enough crowd collects the snake charmer will give a performance.

He seems to be satisfied with his audience now. He sets his baskets down and sits cross-legged on the ground close in front of them. Then he begins to play weird, crooning music on his pipes. The watchers stand or sit around just a few feet away. After a little, the snake

The white neck marking gives these snakes the name of
Spectacled Cobras.

charmer takes off the covers of the baskets with the end of a stick—and at once several heads and bodies rear up. Each neck is flattened out and distended into a hood. On the back of each neck is a prominent white marking that looks like two great eyes behind a pair of spectacles. Now the snake charmer plays faster, swaying his body to the music. The cobras sway, too. They look as if they are dancing in time to the music. And that is the impression the snake charmer wants to give. Actually the snakes don't even hear the music—they are following the swaying of his body.

One snake, gliding from the basket, coils beside the snake charmer's leg and rears up its head and a third of its body. It sways and sways. The man shows not the slightest fear of the serpents. His eyes may not even be upon them. He may be solemnly watching the audience. And the onlookers show no fear either. They have perfect confidence that the snake charmer is in absolute control of the death-dealing serpents just a few feet away from them.

How is it done?

The snake charmers do not hypnotize the snakes. And certainly the men are not immune to the cobra's poison, though it is said they try to make themselves so by swallowing some of the venom or rubbing it on their limbs. True, often the fangs of the cobras have been pulled. But even so the snakes are dangerous because venom flows from the wounds, and if the snake bites with its other teeth, the poison can get into the blood stream. The snake charmer's art is something we don't really understand. All we know is that it takes a lot of nerve to be a snake charmer!

A curious thing about the Spectacled Cobra is that in some regions snakes of this species can *spit* venom. That is, they can force the venom out of the fangs and squirt it at the enemy. You might ask what good that does since venom cannot hurt unless it gets in a cut. That is not quite true. If it gets in the eyes, it blinds you— though not permanently if prompt care is given—and the snake generally aims at the eyes.

The Egyptian Cobra is a very noted cobra. For it was the symbol of royalty in ancient Egypt, and a golden, bejeweled cobra usually ornamented the center of the crown. The Egyptian Cobra is not a spitter. But the Blacknecked Cobra of central Africa is. This snake's aim is better than that of the Spectacled Cobra. But the best spitter of all is the Ringhals Cobra. Not more than three or four feet long, the Ringhals can spit both

The Rhinghals Cobra rears up its body to form a hood.

straight and far. When annoyed, it rears up the front part of its body to form a hood. Then quick as a wink it spits out two jets of venom, aimed right at the eyes. The jets may reach to a distance of six to twelve feet, depending on the size of the snake. And the snake may spit ten or twenty times in rapid succession.

Spitting venom is a fine defense against big birds and mammals. The Ringhals is so good a spitter that it is often called the Spitting Cobra. It is the only cobra that bears living young.

The largest of all the cobras—and also the world's biggest poisonous snake—is the King Cobra of India, Siam, Indo-China, Malaya, and the Philippine Islands. King Cobras grow to eighteen feet and are thorough-going cannibals—they eat almost nothing but snakes. And most of these are Kraits, which belong to their own family.

Kraits are much dreaded in the Orient. These serpents, showily marked with black and white or black and yellow cross bands, are commonly found on cultivated land and in houses, where they are always unwelcome. For while their venom is not so potent as that of the cobras, it is usually fatal to man. So the King Cobra performs a real service by feeding on Kraits.

Venom Is Their Weapon

The famous Mambas are tree snakes that live only in Africa. Some are green, some black. The longest is about twelve feet, and all are narrow and fast-moving. They are very innocent-looking snakes with their slender bodies and large eyes. But don't let that deceive you. A Mamba is deadly poisonous and swift to strike. It will be lying quietly on a branch. A sudden movement, and it will shoot down like a bolt of lightning and sink in its fangs. The fangs are short, the bite is shallow, but the venom is as bad as any there is and works very fast. It has to if the snake is to capture its food. For the Mamba feeds on birds, tree lizards, and other fast-moving creatures. If the venom didn't work rapidly, the prey would get away and out of reach before it died.

Of all the continents, Australia is the most infested with venomous snakes. The Death Adder, the Tiger Snakes, and the Australian Black Snake are very dangerous. The venom of our own Coral Snakes is also dangerous but we are lucky in that we have just two species in our country and both are very secretive.

Our Coral Snakes can always be distinguished from others by the arrangement of bands of black, yellow and red. Milk Snakes, along with some of the King Snakes, are often confused with Coral Snakes. One sure way of telling a harmless snake from a Coral Snake is by the color pattern. Coral Snakes have the red bands bordered by yellow or creamy white bands. The harmless ones have the red bands bordered by black bands. The bands are repeated in this manner:

Coral Snake	Yellow	Red	Yellow	Black	Yellow
Harmless	Black	Red	Black	Yellow	Black

But once in a great while a Coral Snake will show up that is almost completely black. A woman in Texas picked up one such abnormally patterned snake. It bit her on the finger. Within a minute pain swept her whole arm, and soon it spread over the entire body. The woman did not die, but it was four days before she recovered.

14

Sea Serpents—
Imaginary and Real

Over three-quarters of the earth lies the ocean. It is five miles deep in places. Is it not possible that somewhere under that vast expanse of water strange sea monsters lurk?

There has probably been no time when people did not think so. Sailors and fishermen were always coming home with thrilling tales of sea serpents they had seen. There was one, they claimed, that had a head like a horse. It was six hundred feet long and would rear up as high as a ship's mast. When it hissed, it sounded like the tempest. Those who met with it sailed straight toward the sun so that the bright light should blind the serpent.

Always the creatures which mariners had seen were huge. There were tales of squid so gigantic that when lying motionless half out of the water they looked like floating islands. Sailors had rowed up and landed on them—when suddenly the "islands" had given way. There were tales also of enormous whales. Sindbad, the great traveler of the *Arabian Nights*, had mistaken such a whale for an island and had landed on it, with disastrous results.

Now, it is true that there are huge sea creatures unknown to most of us. There *is* a giant squid that grows to fifty feet. Yet it is very doubtful there is any creature unknown to science that ever comes to the surface where people can see it.

"But," you may say, "the ocean is so big and so deep. There *might* be some huge prehistoric monsters down there. And maybe once in a while one of them does come up and sailors see it."

That is quite improbable. Many amazing creatures, large and small, have been dredged up from the dark depths of the ocean. All these beings are specially adapted to the terrific pressure of the miles of water above them. When an animal of the lower depths is brought to the surface, it bursts because the pressure up here is so much less. No, if there is a prehistoric monster hidden among the ledges of the great undersea mountains, it can never come up to the surface—not even for a minute.

Nevertheless there are sea serpents. They are not so enormous that they can swallow a sailing vessel—which is what people sometimes thought happened when a ship failed to return—but they are serpents that live in the sea. The largest of them is about eight feet long, while most measure no more than a yard. In the Indian Ocean and the South Pacific there are a great many sea snakes, and fishermen in those regions often find them in their nets. Some of the snakes look much like eels. But eels,

Often fishermen catch sea snakes in their nets.

of course, have a smooth, slimy skin, whereas serpents have a scaly skin. In the New World there is just one kind—the Yellow-Bellied Sea Snake—living off the west coast of Mexico, Central and South America. In the Atlantic Ocean there is none at all.

The whole family is different from other snakes in that all the sea snakes have nostrils set on top of their heads and a tail shaped like a paddle. Not all, however, live far out at sea. Some come so close to shore that they get into native houses built over the water by climbing up the poles. Many inhabit the mouths of rivers, and some will go as far as a hundred miles up a large river. One kind lives in a salt-water lake in the Solomon Islands. Strangely enough, another is found in a fresh-water lake—in the Philippines.

Sea snakes have no gills so they have to come to the surface to breathe. Thus people on steamers often see them, sometimes in schools of several dozen or more. At night they are attracted to the boat's lights. The creatures are gaily colored, many with bright bands that give the body a ringed look. Storms often wash the sea serpents ashore, and quite often numbers of them will be found on crowded bathing beaches. Yet there is no known case of anyone's being bitten while swimming.

Sea snakes are all venomous, and like their relatives, the cobras, have short, hollow, rigid fangs in the front of the upper jaw. Not all sea snakes, however, have equally potent venom. Fishermen handle some of the serpents very carelessly. Certain kinds are even caught on hook and line as if they were eels, and over much of the Oriental region are used for food.

On land, sea snakes have a hard time of it. One group manages with great difficulty to crawl ashore just to lay eggs. The rest, which bear living young, are so helpless on land that they can reach the low-lying islands only during high tide. When the water recedes, they are left stranded on the land, and there can give birth to their babies.

15

Vipers

Cobras, mambas, coral snakes, sea snakes—all of them have short, hollow, rigid fangs in the front part of the mouth. But now we come to snakes which have *long* hollow fangs in the front part of the upper jaws. And there is something peculiar about these jaws—they can move so that when the mouth is closed, the fangs *fold back against the roof*. We call such snakes vipers. Vipers that have a deep pit between the eye and the nostril are called pit-vipers.

There are no vipers in the entire New World and none in Australia. Europe and Asia have some. But Africa is where they abound—Africa is headquarters for the viper family.

'Way back we mentioned that England has just three kinds of snakes. Of the three the commonest is the Common Viper, or Adder as it is called there. This snake is found in many different kinds of places throughout the British Isles—in lowlands and highlands, in dry places, and in marshy country. And not only in the British Isles. This little snake—it is under two feet long—is so adaptable that it has made itself at home all the way from England to the east coast of Asia. It ranges farther north than any other venomous snake. It lives in the Alps 9,000 feet above sea level.

The Common Viper is very easy to recognize by the zigzag dark line that runs from the neck to the tip of the tail. But—and this is very rare among snakes—the colors of the male and female are different. Male Adders are usually a light cream, yellow or gray with jet-black markings while females are reddish-brown with the markings a darker red or brown.

When you see an Adder lying basking in the sun, as it loves to do, the little snake doesn't look much like a fighter. But male Adders often do fight among themselves when one comes on the territory of another. Facing each other, the heads and foreparts of their bodies held straight up off the ground, they push and shove

Male Adders fight among themselves.

each other until one drops to the ground and leaves. Against human beings they are not aggressive. Indeed, Adders are said to be timid—which is fortunate, for the bite of an Adder can be serious if not treated immediately.

Much more serious, and very often fatal, is the bite of Russell's Viper of India. This snake is also not large —usually it is under four feet—but is is responsible for a third of the deaths from snake bite in that country. It lives in all kinds of situations except dense jungle and is so common in some places that over 450 were caught in a single day. Because they are great rat eaters, these snakes are found around houses, sometimes right in the middle of a town.

Russell's Viper is frequently one of the serpents the snake charmer carries around with him. The onlookers recognize it at once by its three rows of large oval spots, for they know the snake well. There is always anxiety when it crawls from the basket toward the snake charmer.

The vipers of Africa have even more different habitats than the vipers of Europe and Asia. Some live in the desert, some in the jungle, and some underground. Most famous of all is the Gaboon Viper. It is the largest and heaviest of all vipers, growing to nearly six feet. If you measured its width as it rests on the ground, it might be six inches. The head might be as large as a man's fist. And the fangs would be the longest you would find in any snake at all—an inch and three quarters long.

The Gaboon Viper, which some people think hideous and some handsome, has a thick body with a light and dark velvety looking splotched pattern. This makes it difficult to see the snake on the fallen leaves of the sunlit forest floor. But luckily for the natives, the snake is not aggressive, so that bites are very rare.

Another famous viper is the Saw-scaled Viper that is found both in Africa and Asia. I had the opportunity of seeing this pale brown desert dweller in captivity at close range. The creature is just a little one, less than three feet long. When it is disturbed, it throws itself into a double coil like a figure eight with the head in the center. Then it rubs the coils against each other. That sets up a rustling, hissing sound because the scales on the snake's sides are saw-toothed. An authority on the snakes of Ceylon calls the Saw-scaled Viper the most vicious snake of the region. It will bite on the slightest provocation. And the venom of this small creature is supposed to be sixteen times more potent than that of Russell's Viper!

The scales of a Saw-scaled Viper make a hissing sound as they
rub against each other.

16

Pit-Vipers

Most of the vipers are in the Old World, but with pit-vipers it is just the other way. There are a few in southeast Asia, Malaya, and part of Indonesia, and there is one species in Russia. But you find the biggest and most varied kinds in North and South America.

The pit between the eye and the nostril puts all these snakes into one family. They have some other things in common, too. All the pit-vipers have a flat, triangular head, very distinct from the neck. And in most of them the top of the head is covered with small scales.

As for the fangs which are so important to these snakes, they are long as in vipers, and the mechanism is always in working order. At intervals the old fangs are replaced by new ones. However, an old fang is never shed until the new one has grown in. It grows in right *beside* the old fang and becomes connected with the poison duct. Then, when the new fang is fully grown, the snake sheds the old fang.

Rattlesnakes are the most truly American pit-vipers, for rattlers are found only in this hemisphere. Early travelers in the New World were deeply impressed with this serpent and brought frightening tales of the creature back to Europe. Rattlesnakes were *the* horror of the American wilderness, they reported. The snakes were thirty feet long, they said, gave forth poisonous vapors

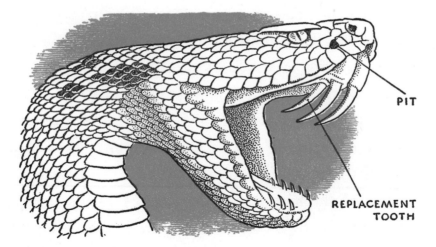

PIT

REPLACEMENT
TOOTH

The pit-viper has a pit between the eye and nostril.

from the mouth, and had something at the end of the tail that looked like a bell!

This certainly is a wild description of rattlers, the largest of which doesn't grow beyond nine feet. The poisonous vapors are, of course, nonsense. And the bell-like structure at the end of the tail can scarcely be called a portrait of the famous rattle.

Let us pause a moment to consider this rattle, which no other snake in the world possesses. What is it for? And how does it grow?

We say the rattlesnake "warns" that it is going to strike its prey. But that surely cannot be what the rattle was developed for. It doesn't *help* the snake to warn its prey. More likely the rattle is a warning device to "frighten" the *enemy* away.

A baby rattler is born with a soft button at the end of its tail. After a few days the little snake sheds its skin and starts to eat and grow. It grows fast. In a few months it sheds its skin again. It is then that the first ring, or segment, of the rattle comes into view—just above the button. The ring is soft and fits loosely on the base of the button. In a few days the ring is dry, and now when the rattler shakes his tail, there is a faint little buzz. The noise is caused by the rasping of the

You hear a faint buzz when the rattler shakes his tail.

button against the loosely attached ring. The next time
the snake sheds its skin, another and bigger rattle ap-
pears, fitting loosely over the base of the one below.
Now the snake can really rattle. And so the rattle keeps
on increasing, a ring at each shedding.

In the United States there are fifteen kinds of rattlesnakes. The Eastern Diamond-backed Rattler is the
largest, growing to nearly nine feet, although the average is about five. This species lives in the lowlands from
North Carolina south to Florida and west to Louisiana.

In southern Florida it is very common, and there I have found many dead ones on the highways—killed by automobiles. The Western Diamond-backed Rattler is somewhat similar in color pattern except that it has white and black rings on its tail. This snake, which doesn't grow beyond seven feet, is usually found in dry areas of the middle Southwest. Then in California there is the Red Diamond-backed Rattler. Except that it is redder in color, it is very similar to its cousin of the Southwest.

It is not the Diamondback but the Timber or Banded Rattlesnake that is common in the Northeast. This species averages only about two feet long, but in the South, where it is called the Canebrake Rattler, it grows bigger—up to six feet. Mice, squirrels, rabbits, shrews and small birds are their fare. These snakes tend to hibernate in a single den together with Black Snakes and Copperheads.

In the eastern part of our country rattlers are dwindling down to a colony here and another one there. This is bound to go on as the suburbs grow. On Long Island there isn't a single one left of all the Timber Rattlers that once were there—as long ago as 1916 the last one was killed. And this is too bad because it was a peculiar type and it has now been exterminated. So far as I know, only one specimen of this type has ever been preserved. It is now in the Brooklyn Children's Museum.

In the grasslands the Prairie Rattler is the common one. It lives all over the West as far as the eastern border of the Great Plains. It likes best to hibernate in rock outcrops and crevices, but if there aren't any around, it will use empty rodent burrows.

One of the most peculiar of the rattlers is the Horned Rattlesnake or Sidewinder. This desert dweller of Cali-

The tracks of a Sidewinder show that it moves sideways.

fornia, Arizona, Nevada, and Mexico gets the name "Sidewinder" from the queer way in which it travels when it wants to get somewhere in a hurry. At other times it moves in a straight line as other snakes do. But when it wants to go fast, instead of throwing its body from side to side and wriggling along, it throws its body into a sort of S-shape and travels sideways. When you look at its tracks, you see a series of them, each one completely separate from the others.

There is another group of snakes in the world that moves like this. It is a group of African desert vipers. Curiously enough, like the Sidewinder, they also have a horned projection over the eye.

Rattlesnakes aren't always big or even middle-sized. Several in our Southwest are dwarfs no more than two or two and a half feet long, with rattles so small that they make a sound like a very faint electric buzzer. One dwarf lives in the Southeast. It is called the Pygmy Rattlesnake and is only eighteen inches long.

In our country we have two kinds of pit-vipers that aren't rattlesnakes—the copperhead and the moccasin. The copperhead gets its name because its head, which is usually a paler tint than the body, often has a coppery tinge. Though it is not an aggressive snake and generally runs away when it is discovered, it is camouflaged by its pattern. Because you may not see the creature in the fallen leaves, you may easily step on it. It is only about two and a half feet long. This is the same snake that in some areas is called Upland Moccasin or Chunk-head.

Copperheads may not collect in such large or conspicuous hibernation dens as rattlesnakes and so are harder to get rid of. In many areas where the rattler has disappeared, the copperhead still lives on. Even in the past few years I have seen copperheads in a wilderness area overlooking the heart of New York City.

The copperhead is one of the American pit-vipers.

All About Snakes

Neither the local people nor the thousands of commuters who pass by each day suspect the creatures are there, so close to them.

Copperheads are very different from moccasins, yet the babies of both look so much alike that you might confuse them. Usually, however, you can tell a baby moccasin by the place where you find it. For moccasins are water-loving creatures. I have often seen them basking on logs or stumps in swamps and along sluggish streams in the South. When I would disturb one, it would generally draw back its head and open its mouth wide. Then I would see the white lining which gives the creature its other name—Cotton Mouth.

Central and South America have pit-vipers larger than any of ours. The Bushmaster, which is the only pit-viper that lays eggs, is known to reach nine feet in length. In the same general area lives also the Fer-de-lance. It is the second largest pit-viper. This snake likes to stay on cultivated land where it can get plenty of rats and other mammals to eat, and on account of this habit it is often a great danger, especially to workers in the sugar-cane fields. For the snake multiplies very fast. It is not at all uncommon for a Fer-de-lance to give birth to seventy babies all at one time.

17

Fighting to Live

Snakes eat other snakes. But are cannibals the only enemies snakes have?

Far from it. It has enemies among the mammals, among reptiles, birds, fish, and even among insects.

In the warmer parts of the world small mammals frequently prey on snakes. Skunks even hunt for snake nests so as to feast on the eggs. Mink, foxes, raccoons, and opossum include snakes in their diet. Rats destroy many. In Europe the hedgehog is an important snake enemy —it is even immune to the venom of the Common Viper. But of all the small mammals the mongoose is the most famous killer. Although mongooses are not immune to venom, they attack poisonous as well as harmless snakes. Tales of battles between cobra and mongoose have been greatly exaggerated. The mongoose is not always the victor.

I saw many mongooses when I was in the West Indies. The animals had been introduced into the islands to kill the venomous snakes and the rats. Unfortunately, several species of harmless snakes were exterminated, and the mongooses themselves became a pest. In Jamaica they were very common. While driving around I often saw them run across the road, the way rabbits do here.

Among the birds, the large Secretary Bird of Africa is a great snake enemy. It kills snakes with its powerful feet. Birds of prey sometimes swoop down on a snake, soar with it over a rock, and drop the serpent to its death. Then they devour it. Certain other large birds kill snakes with their sharp beaks. Sea birds eat sea snakes.

Alligators, crocodiles, certain lizards, and even some frogs prey on snakes. Sharks and other large fish eat sea snakes. So do some whales. At the other end of the animal world, spiders kill snakes and suck their juices.

But from the snake's point of view, public enemy number one is man. He destroys millions of snakes every

Birds of prey sometimes swoop down and devour a snake.

year. He hunts them for their skin; he dynamites them in their dens. He kills them just to kill them. In many places he is exterminating them. His automobile especially is a menace to snakes, particularly at dusk and at night; for snakes are attracted to the warm asphalt of roads as night approaches and the air gets cooler. One scientist has estimated that in San Diego County, California, 10,000 snakes are killed by cars every year.

Against man snakes have almost no defense except their venom. And against man's automobiles and dynamite they have no defense at all. But against others of their enemies many snakes have developed protective devices and habits. Here are some of them:

The simple fact that snakes look the way they do is often protection enough—their color and form blend with their background so that the creatures are hard to see. Scientists call this camouflage *protective coloration*. The copperhead, whose pattern is like the fallen leaves of the forest floor is an example of it. The Green Snake, which is the color of leaves, is another. Many of the desert snakes are pale-colored like the sand on which they live.

Some of the venomous snakes are protected by their very bright color, which speaks for the snake, saying,

"Beware! I am a dangerous creature!" We call this *warning coloration*. One of the best examples of it is our Coral Snakes. They are burrowers and secretive animals, yet they are vivid with red, black, and yellow cross bands. The bright colors warn their enemies, such as birds, to leave Coral Snakes alone.

Some snakes which are quite harmless often resemble dangerous snakes in color and pattern. This is a protective device which took millions of years to develop. The harmless snake, without knowing it, *mimics* the coloration of the venomous snake, and enemies fear and leave both of them alone. Thus the southern Milk Snake often escapes death because it resembles the Coral Snake. In the North, where there are no Coral Snakes, the Milk Snake does not resemble them at all.

Again, there are snakes which use bright color to *startle* the enemy. The Ringnecked Snake, for instance, will often flash the bright red, orange, or yellow underside of its tail when annoyed.

With many snakes the first defense measure is to flee. But not all snakes do that when approached. Some will coil up into a small ball, hiding the head in the middle of the coil, and so making themselves harder to pick up. Others merely hide their heads under a coil. When the venomous Krait of India does this, he may turn and bite the animal that is so foolhardy as to try to pick him up.

Another defense measure is to make a noise. Some snakes hiss. Hissing makes them appear more threatening. Cobras hiss so that they can be heard seventy-five feet away. Rattling the tail is another threatening noise. Many harmless snakes rattle their tails against the ground. The common Black Snake does this often and when the rattling is done against dry leaves, you might think a rattlesnake was near. But, of course, the rattler puts on the best performance in this line.

Besides hissing, some snakes have additional threatening tricks. The cobra raises a hood. The Hog-nosed Snake puffs himself up by filling his lungs with air. If this doesn't have any effect, he will broaden and flatten his body so that he looks bigger. If the enemy still isn't scared off, the snake will roll over on his back with mouth open and tongue hanging out as if he were dead.

Several of the boas of the West Indies use an especially startling way of defending themselves when picked up. Their eyes become red and blood oozes out of the mouth and nostrils. This blood doesn't clot like

Often the Black Snake makes a noise like a rattler by vibrating its tail against dry leaves.

ordinary blood but remains liquid for a long time. It is not a poisonous bloody secretion, but it may be distasteful to the enemy and is certainly annoying to the person who tries to handle it.

Many other snakes protect themselves with a nasty-smelling excretion. By emptying their scent glands, they can make it unpleasant for the enemy who picks them up. Water and Garter Snakes do this readily, and one learns quickly to hold the tail of these snakes away when handling them.

18

Your Snake Pet

"But," you may ask, "why shouldn't man kill snakes? What's the good of a snake?"

Now, we have said a lot of hard things about snakes. We have pointed out that many are dangerous and that man must beware of them. But we have also said that most of the world's snakes are harmless. One herpetologist estimated that only one in twelve need be greatly feared. Why should we kill harmless kinds just because we fear dangerous ones? Man's unreasonable hatred of snakes is such that he will kill a snake on sight—just because it is a snake. "There's a snake! Kill it!" is most people's attitude. Many will even go out of their way to kill one. Often when I have found a dead snake on the highway, I could tell by the tire tracks that people had crossed over on purpose to drive over the snake.

It is this senseless attitude that herpetologists would like to see changed. They would like people to get over their unreasoning hatred of snakes, most of which—especially in this country—are harmless and many of which are useful to man.

Their greatest usefulness lies in the fact that lots of them eat rats, mice, gophers and other rodents. These animals are very destructive to certain of our food crops—particularly grain crops—and snakes that eat them

Many a snake helps the farmer by devouring rats and mice.

should be encouraged, not stamped out. A rodent-eating snake means so many dollars and cents to the farmer. Some of our farmers are beginning to realize this and with great good sense, instead of killing Bull Snakes, are introducing them on their acres.

In countries where that dread disease bubonic plague is a frequent occurrence, even dangerous snakes may be protected if they eat rats; for rats are the spreaders of this disease—their fleas are the carriers of the Black Death which once killed off a quarter of England's population.

Snakes are useful to man in other ways. In some parts of the world they supply food. We ourselves are not a snake-eating people, but even we are making discoveries in this line—rattlesnake meat is being canned as a great delicacy. Snake skins, however, have more value for us and for the rest of the world. In the making of shoes, handbags, bill folds, and so on, many thousands of dollars' worth of snake skins are used.

In recent years science has made an exciting discovery that puts even some dangerous snakes on the useful list. Doctors have learned that venom can heal as well as kill. The poison of several venomous snakes is being successfully used as medicine.

The fact that a creature has no legs, no fur, no feathers is no reason to kill it. And I am glad to say that more and more people are coming around to this point of view. They are getting over an age-old prejudice. They are even discovering that snakes make delightful pets.

Not all the harmless snakes make equally good ones, of course. You would not want to get a burrower, for instance—he would burrow out of sight and you'd not see him except at night. Nor would you want a snake that eats things you would find hard to supply. The common Hog-nosed Snake doesn't ask for much—he prefers toads. This seems like an easy thing to get, and so you would find it, but not in all seasons of the year. The Pygmy Boa might tempt you, for it is a very attractive creature. But it eats lizards that will be hard to get if you live in the North. Some animal dealers might get you excited about a boa, which also makes an attractive and interesting pet. But this boa requires living mice and rats.

The common Garter Snake is an ideal snake to keep. It isn't fussy about food. It will eat either soft grubs, or earthworms, or frogs, or salamanders. A diet like that is easy to supply. In fact, the Garter Snake's food can be still less of a problem if you mix chopped meat with its earthworms. Gradually you can reduce the amount of earthworms until the snake will eat chopped meat whenever it is offered.

Many other native snakes will do just as well in captivity as the Garter Snake. The Yellow Chicken Snake and its cousin the Pilot Black Snake make excellent pets. They will feed readily on mice and may eat them even if these aren't alive. It is often better to feed such snakes on laboratory-raised animals because there is less chance of parasites and diseases. These two snakes are also favorites because many of them will feed on eggs, the larger specimens often take small chicken eggs.

Proper housing for your snake pet is not hard to provide. For most species a small cage is fine. But make sure your box is escape-proof because snakes are experts at getting out of the best of cages. The smallest crack into which a head can be wedged is all a snake needs to escape. However, in building your cage, take care to leave a few *small* cracks or crevices so that you can thoroughly drain the cage after it has been cleaned and washed. Most snake owners put a screen front on the cage. A screen provides good ventilation and makes it easy to observe the pet. But if you have a screen, be sure to use wire which has no sharp edges. For many snakes while

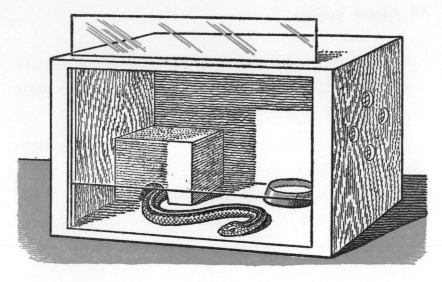

Glass makes a good front for a snake cage.

exploring their quarters rub their noses against the screen and injure their scales. This leaves places open to infection. In fact, it is probably better to use a glass front, particularly if the glass can be made to slide up and down.

A thing you must give thought to is temperature. If you keep your snake at a temperature under 70 degrees Fahrenheit, it will become inactive, will not feed, and will soon waste away. A temperature between 75 and 80 degrees will be just right. You must also remember that a snake needs a little water to drink. A small shallow dish placed inside the cage will supply all the drinking water the snake needs. As for feeding, a good meal two to four times a month is enough.

All About Snakes

After a few feedings, most snakes will show signs of shedding. Usually a milky color will appear on the scale covering the eye. The skin all over the snake will also become much duller. You may find your pet irritable at this time. After a few days, the milky appearance of the eyes will disappear and the skin will become clear again. At this point the snake is ready for shedding. Usually he needs more moist conditions at this time. Some snakes will sit in a bowl of water, others will prefer a wet cloth sack. You should provide one or the other and also a stone or some rough object for him to rub his snout against so he can loosen the skin around it.

Most snakes are secretive creatures. They fear sudden motions and like to hide beneath or behind objects. Many snake keepers have noted that a snake lives longer if it can find a hiding place. You can easily provide one. All you need do is place a small cardboard box in the cage. Put the box open side down and cut a small notch in its walls so that the snake can crawl in.

I must warn you about one thing—parasites that suck the snake's blood and spread infectious disease. The parasites are called mites. Many of the snakes recently captured in the wild are infested with them, and your snake may have them, too. Mites are very tiny, only about a fiftieth of an inch long. Look for them along the edges of the scales, for that is where they hide. In order to get rid of these pests, it may be necessary to wash the snake in a mild insecticide and to keep the body under water so as to drown the mites. It is important also to clean and disinfect the cage thoroughly.

Mites are about the only trouble you are likely to have with your snake, and these are no worse than the fleas your dog or cat is apt to have. On the whole you will find your snake pet very easy to care for—much easier than a mammal or a bird. Your snake will not have to be fed or watered every day. You won't have to bathe it. It will not get lonesome. You will be able to go away a week or more at a time and come back to find it as well and contented as ever. It will make a clean, graceful, interesting pet that will give you little trouble and much pleasure for many years.

Index

Index

Index

About the Author of This Book

BESSIE M. HECHT, a native New Yorker, developed an enthusiastic interest in biology while in high school. While attending Hunter College, she became interested in herpetology, and during one summer vacation worked as a volunteer in the Staten Island Zoo which has one of the best snake collections in the country. Later she joined the staff of the Department of Amphibians and Reptiles at the American Museum of Natural History, where she was engaged in research, cared for living and preserved reptiles and amphibians, and answered public inquiries concerning these unusual animals.

With her zoologist husband, who is an instructor at Queens College, Mrs. Hecht has collected snakes and other reptiles, and amphibians for the Museum on numerous trips in many parts of the United States, Canada and the West Indies. Now, besides doing some work in paleontology and popular science writing, she is busy with her small daughter who helps her care for their home reptile zoo that includes a baby boa, three garter snakes, a chicken snake, some frogs, turtles, lizards and even a baby crocodile.

About the Illustrator of This Book

RUDOLF FREUND has become known as one of the outstanding wildlife artists in America today. This distinguished career began just after high school when young Freund, who had planned to become a scientific farmer, was awarded a four-year scholarship to the Philadelphia School of Industrial Art. His father persuaded him to try it and art has been his absorbing interest ever since.

For a number of years Rudolf Freund was on the staff of the American Museum of Natural History where he had the opportunity to make hundreds of wildlife sketches on field trips with leading scientists. By this time he has illustrated countless books and field guides on wild life. His lavish full-color illustrations for the various science features of *Life Magazine* have won him worldwide recognition.